P9-CCZ-102

A Character Building Book™

Learning About Honesty from the Life of
Abraham Lincoln

Kiki Mosher

The Rosen Publishing Group's
PowerKids Press™
New York

FRANKLIN PIERCE
COLLEGE LIBRARY
RINDGE, N.H. 03461

Published in 1996 by The Rosen Publishing Group, Inc.
29 East 21st Street, New York, NY 10010

Copyright © 1996 by The Rosen Publishing Group, Inc.

All rights reserved. No part of this book may be reproduced in any form without permission in writing from the publisher, except by a reviewer.

First Edition

Book design: Erin McKenna

Photo credits: Cover © Archive Photos; pp. 4, 8, 11, 12, 16, 19, 20 © The Bettmann Archive; pp. 7, 15 © Corbis-Bettmann.

Mosher, Kiki.
    Learning about honesty from the life of Abraham Lincoln / by Kiki Mosher.
        p.   cm. — (A character building book)
    Includes index.
    ISBN 0-8239-2420-3
    Summary: Extolls the virtue of honesty through examples in the life of Abraham Lincoln.
    1.Lincoln, Abraham, 1809–1865—Juvenile literature. 2. Presidents—United States—Biography—Juvenile literature. 3. Honesty—Juvenile literature. [1. Lincoln, Abraham, 1809–1865. 2. Presidents. 3. Honesty.] I. Title. II. Series.
    E457.905M68 1996
    973.7'092—dc20   96-15666
                                                                                    CIP
                                                                                    AC

CURR
E
457.905
M68
.1996

Manufactured in the United States of America

Table of Contents

1   The 16th President   5
2   Childhood   6
3   Learning   9
4   Honest Abe   10
5   Abe's Own Store   13
6   Abe's Law Career   14
7   Interest in Politics   17
8   Slavery   18
9   The Civil War   21
10 The End of Slavery   22
    Glossary   23
    Index   24

The 16th President

Abraham Lincoln was one of the most popular presidents of the United States. One of the main reasons he was so admired was because of his **honesty** (ON-es-tee).

Abe was always gentle and patient when dealing with people. He always tried to be fair and to do the right thing. He is remembered as "Honest Abe," loved and respected by everyone.

◀ *Abraham Lincoln was considered a good, kind, and honest man by many people across the United States.*

Childhood

Abe was born near Hodgenville, Kentucky, in 1809. His parents were farmers who moved often while Abe and his sister were growing up. The family was very poor. They grew their own food and made their own clothes and tools. The children helped around the house and in the fields. As a young boy, Abe had to plow the fields, carry water, chop wood, and plant and harvest corn. Life was not easy. But Abe worked hard and never complained.

Abe was poor growing up. He and his family lived in small cabins such as this one. ▶

Learning

Winter was the only time that Abe and his sister could go to school. This was because there wasn't as much work to be done on the farm. Abe loved school, but he could go only for a few winters. He was very curious, so he continued to study on his own. He read everything he could get his hands on.

Abe continued to study and learn new things throughout his life.

◀ *Abe read as much as he could.*
He often read by firelight.

Honest Abe

When Abe was 21, he left home and moved to New Salem, Illinois. There he worked splitting logs into rails for train tracks. He also worked as a store clerk.

One day at the store, a customer forgot to pick up her change. Abe didn't notice until long after she had left the store. She lived several miles away. But Abe thought it was important for her to have her change. After work, he walked many miles to reach her house to return her change. From then on he was known as "Honest Abe."

When Abe first moved away from home, he worked splitting railroad ties. ▶

Abe's Own Store

A few months later, Abe and one of his friends borrowed some money to buy a store of their own. Farmers brought their products to Abe's store to be sold. They knew they would always get a fair price from him.

Soon after the store opened, Abe's partner and friend died. Abe couldn't afford to keep the store by himself, but he still owed the money that they borrowed. So he worked at several jobs. It took him many years, but he paid back every single dollar. After that, people respected Abe even more.

◄ *Abe took many jobs, including running a type of ferry called a flatboat, to pay off his debt.*

Abe's Law Career

Abe had always been interested in honesty, fairness, and **justice** (JUS-tis). He began to study law as a way of bringing justice to all. He studied hard and visited the courthouse often. Finally, he became a lawyer. He opened his own law office.

He was very successful. People everywhere knew that Abe **represented** (rep-ree-ZEN-tid) only people that he believed were innocent, or people whose **rights** (RYTS) were not being **upheld** (up-HELD).

Abe enjoyed working with people as a lawyer. ▶

Interest in Politics

Abe also wanted to be a **politician** (pol-ih-TISH-un). People voted for him because they trusted him and believed in his honesty. He was elected to the Illinois state **legislature** (LEH-jis-lay-cher) in 1834, when he was 25 years old. Twelve years later, he was elected to the U.S. **Congress** (KON-gress). He fought for equal rights for all people.

Finally, in 1860, Abe was elected President of the United States.

◄ *This photograph shows Abraham Lincoln being sworn in as President of the United States.*

17

Slavery

Even before he was president, Abraham Lincoln opposed **slavery** (SLAY-ver-ree). Slavery was the practice of allowing some people to "own" others. Slaves were forced to work long hours with little rest or food. They received no pay for their work. They were beaten if they did not follow orders. Slaves had no freedom and no rights.

In 1860, slavery was allowed in the Southern states. President Lincoln knew slavery was wrong.

Slaves were often sold like animals at markets or auctions. ▶

The Civil War

The Southern states wanted to continue slavery. They were willing to separate from the Northern states to keep the right to own slaves. President Lincoln and the Northern states believed that slavery should end. And they were willing to fight to keep the United States together. For that reason, in 1861, the American Civil War began.

The Civil War lasted until 1865. Meanwhile, in 1864, Lincoln was elected president again.

◄ *For President Lincoln, the Civil War was a fight both to end slavery and to keep the United States together.*

The End of Slavery

In 1865, the North won the Civil War. Slavery was outlawed. And the North and South stayed together. Many people were happy and were proud of the President. But not everyone was.

Five days after the war ended, President Lincoln and his wife went to a play. John Wilkes Booth, who had supported slavery, shot President Lincoln. President Lincoln died the next morning. The country **mourned** (MORND) the loss of Abraham Lincoln, an honest man and a great president.

Glossary

Congress (KON-gress) Group of people who makes laws.

honesty (ON-es-tee) Truthfulness.

justice (JUS-tis) Fairness.

legislature (LEH-jis-lay-cher) Group of people who makes laws.

mourn (MORN) To feel deep sadness.

politician (pol-ih-TISH-un) Person who works in the government.

represent (rep-ree-ZENT) To act or speak for someone or something else in a court of law.

rights (RYTS) Equal treatment.

slavery (SLAY-ver-ree) Practice of allowing some people to "own" others.

upheld (up-HELD) Having something supported or defended.

Index

B
Booth, John Wilkes, 22

C
childhood, 6
Civil War, 21, 22
Congress, 17

F
farm, life on, 6, 9

H
"Honest Abe," 5, 10
honesty, 5, 10, 14, 17, 22

L
law, study of, 14
legislature, 17

P
politician, 17
president, 5, 17, 18, 21, 22

S
school, 9
slavery, 18, 21
 outlawed, 22
store, opened, 13

24

FRANKLIN PIERCE COLLEGE LIBRARY

00105603

DATE DUE

MAR 0 7 '99		
MAR 2 5 '99		
MAY 0 8		
DEC 2 1 2000		
MAR 0 1 2004		
GAYLORD		PRINTED IN U.S.A